Grippy Socks

Grippy Socks

Poems by

Dory Warner

© 2026 Dory Warner. All rights reserved.
This material may not be reproduced in any form, published,
reprinted, recorded, performed, broadcast,
rewritten or redistributed without
the explicit permission of Dory Warner.
All such actions are strictly prohibited by law.

Cover design by Shay Culligan
Cover image by Mariola Grobelska on Unsplash

ISBN: 978-1-63980-823-6
Library of Congress Control Number: 2025951498

Kelsay Books
502 South 1040 East, A-119
American Fork, Utah 84003
Kelsaybooks.com

*For and in loving memory of my Buba, June Factor,
who inspired me to wake up the writer that has always
been inside me. Thank you for reminding us
to keep our faces to the sun.*

Acknowledgments

To my brilliant, feisty mom: Thank you for your bottomless love, humor, wisdom, and belief in me, without which I would not have begun to believe in myself. Thank you for putting up with me even when I send you thirty-three versions of the same poem in one night. You are my role model and my guiding light.

To Mary Walsh and my CREA-E 121 classmates: Thank you for jumping into the water with me and delighting in the joy of swimming in our stories. Thank you for allowing me to feel seen as a writer. You incontrovertibly confirmed my passion for writing.

To Norbert: Thank you for the constant snuggles, sniffs, snorts, and overflowing love, without which this collection would not have been written. You make my world go round (and round and round).

Contents

Airborne	11
Razzle Dazzle	12
Back Pocket Crumbs	13
Spinning	14
Grippy Socks	15
We Are There and the Bus Is Not	16
Rerouting	18
Crumb	19
The Creek	20
Dear J	21
Mundane	24
To Every You	25
Gills	26
Write About It	27
Gardening Advice	28
The Art of Running Late	29
A Terribly Not Bad Very Fine Day	30
More Crumbs	31
Every Fairytale	32
Tilted	33
Park Date	34
Crumpled Pieces	35
After the Party I	36
To the boy I thought I was in love with because he wasn't in love with me	37
You	38
Unsharpened Pencils	39
Globus Sensation	40
Every Single Tree	42
Houseguest	43
Sticky Note	44
Tie-Dyed Love	45
Poetry	48

Airborne

Sometimes I am a juggler
who retrieves the thoughts
I toss into the air.

Sometimes I am a person
who drops myself
to see where I will land.

Sometimes I leave
without knowing the destination
only the necessity to depart.

Sometimes I get stuck
between two
ruminations.

Sometimes I look back
and trip over
myself.

Razzle Dazzle

I am both plot
and twist
in the absence of an ending.

I am a poet
bellowing lines
to an empty theater.

I am a comedian
pausing for echoes
and laughing to create more.

I am a magician
vanishing from stage
by swallowing myself whole.

Back Pocket Crumbs

For every door you try.
For every wall that doesn't open.
For every room you run from.
For every crack you fill with yourself.

For everything you see
that reminds you of what you don't.
For everything you write
that reminds you of when you didn't.

For every haunted house
that grins at you in the mirror.
For every time you look at mania
and dissociation looks back.

For every journal you bleed through.
For every empty table you bring nothing to.
For every lust that strangles you.
For every heartbreak that doesn't become a poem.

Spinning

Orange whiskey bong water.
Cough syrup shots.

Upside down corridors.
Slippery memories.

Three steps forward.
Three steps back.

If you want to find me
you will have to get lost.

Grippy Socks

I want to know how tightly you gripped chaos
and how long it took you to slip.
I want to know how deeply you buried yourself
and how long it took you to reach the bottom.

I want to know about the love letters
you didn't receive.
I want to know about the knots
you didn't untangle.

I want to know about the hiding spots
you didn't want to find.
I want to know about the addictions
you didn't want to kick.

I want to know about the memories
you stored yourself in.
I want to know about the rabbit holes
you lost yourself in.

We Are There and the Bus Is Not

Double-check both sides of a zero-part equation,
then the middle.
Once three times is
a trifecta
of balance,
nine times is still three
if three cancels
itself out.

He is 7th grade and handsome year 1,
he is
sitting anywhere at lunch
and
an assembly of oration
and
fragrant conviction
and
an extroverted formula.

I am 8th grade and acne year 2,
I am
where will I sit at lunch
and
a lit mag of unsubmitted words
and
pungent diffidence
and
a blanket term for something.

We are there
and the bus is not.

He is asking why I look
so depressed all the time.
I am asking why he looks
like the absence of a question.

He was the password that always worked.
I was the lockbox that never opened.
He was the whisper that never settled.
I was the silence that gathered dust.

He was not the crime
and he was not the case.
I was the nosedive
and I was the netting.

He was the stained glass that covered the window.
I was the earthquake that lost track of the time.

If we are the past
we were also the present.
If we are here
we were also there.

Dust catches
but so does air.

Rerouting

Be gentle with others,
but not so gentle
you forget the difference
between exploring your mind
and allowing someone inside it.

Be gentle with others,
but not so gentle
you forget the difference
between taking your clothes off
and being stripped bare.

Be gentle with yourself,
but not so gentle
you forget the difference
between numbness
and the static
of your own caress.

Be gentle with yourself,
but not so gentle
you forget the difference
between weathering rage
and continuing in an effort
to weather yourself.

Crumb

For every repressed memory
that comes out of you
as a poem.

The Creek

I am thinking of a love of bananagrams
and a fear of bananas.
I am thinking of an outdoor healing garden
and a door that never led outside.

I am thinking of semi-formal hospital gowns
and obsessions gripped tighter than socks.
I am thinking of first visit steppingstones
and the second visits they led to.

Dear J,

I tend to err
on the side
of diametric opposition.
Purgative words
evoke a familiar nausea
on their way up.
An antithetical palate,
neutralized by acid.
Alkaline is an acquired taste.

It appears there is a reason
there is a word
to describe the door
through which one can exit.
It appears there are words
to describe the thoughts
that have been gathering
acid inside me.
I think you might know the ones
to which I refer—
the thoughts that were words
about the issue not at hand,
the panic about the game
that wasn't being played.

Talk therapy is
not a misnomer,
but you knew that telling
a driven antithetical
to water herself

was the quickest way
to ensure a draught.

You understood in ways
that I pretended to
that growth is always
attached to a root.
You understood that food
was only a vessel
for my larger addiction
to swallowing pain
and coughing up absence.
It appears I spent a decade
throwing up food
to avoid my fear
of throwing up words.

I come from a family of writers.
I wrote all the time as a kid.
It occurred to me I ran the risk
of becoming a cliché,
so I decided
to bury this fear
along with my words.

You were my sun,
who reminded me
that decaying patterns
are meant to be unearthed,

that dissonance
can be cultivated
as consonance's seedling,
that chaos gardeners must confront
the shaded corners
of abandoned gardens.

Recently in
the most relative way,
I decided
to dig myself out.
It occurred to me that this
is the bigger cliché,
so I decided
to write about it.

Mundane

In my search for meaning
the endless mundane
has calmly been waiting.

To Every You

Harmonize strength
to the little girl who steps back
to make the small space
she occupies
less.

Gills

If you are a sweater
I am the thread
that snagged on the nail.

If you are a game
I am the ink
that smudged out the rules.

If you are a punch
I am the line
that became the bag.

If you are a man
I am the apology
that rubbed itself raw.

If you are a fact
I am the figments
that shattered into fiction.

Write About It

Poetry
because mania
loves to play dress up.

Gardening Advice

Compose yourself for decomposition.

Acknowledge the savvy of a misplaced garden shovel
and manicure fingers into claws.

Do not stop digging when the rot comes up.

Buried decay becomes treasure
and you will find it in troves.

Admire the fluency with which nature
speaks every love language.

Whistle affirmations to lambs quarters
when it comes to compete with itself.

Once you meet yourself in rot,
this is the ground you must cover
to get from here to yourself.

The Art of Running Late

If I had not enticed the clock to join me
in another round of hide and seek
perhaps the subway
would not have been recruited
to play for the other team.

If I had not trusted the elevator
to move faster than the stairs
perhaps a fast-paced walk
could have kept up
with my unpaced sprint.

If I had not stopped to check whether the time
had also taken a break
perhaps I would have missed
the smirk of the taillights
rather than the train.

If I had not gone to driving school
to become a pedestrian
perhaps my arrival
would not have collided
with on-time's departure.

If I had not used gambling
with every minute of the clock
to replace anxiety about my destination
perhaps I would not have imperfected
the art of running late.

A Terribly Not Bad Very Fine Day

It will hit you when you had
a Fine day at work
and the crosswalk timers
don't run out
just before you reach them
and the subway car
isn't crowded
and the train
doesn't stall
and isn't running behind
and isn't too hot
or too cold
and there are open seats
and no one is screaming at god
or at nothing
and everything is going
kind of
okay
and then
it will hit you
anyway.

More Crumbs

For every mirror
you don't hide from.

For every word
you don't mumble.

For every staring contest
you don't have with the clock.

Every Fairytale

Once upon a time,
a wolf donned a red hood
and chased herself
through the woods.

Once there was a boy who peed into wine bottles
so no one would notice how much he was drinking.
Once there was a girl who vomited into showers
so no one would notice how much she was puking.

Once there was a boy who fell in love with how the ground looks
right before impact.
Once there was a boy who forgot to take his baggage
on his way out.

Once there was a girl who opened a book
and counted every syllable.
Once there was a girl who wrote so little
she lost her words.

Long ago, in a kingdom far, far, too familiar,
a little girl fell in love
with everything that seemed likely
to not love her back.

Tilted

The irony in my lust
is that when I have sex
they fall for my nudity
but run when I strip down
to my skimpiest thoughts.

The irony in my dissociation
is that I wink at myself
to remind my shadow
that I have always been
both skin and splinter.

The irony in my avoidance
is that I keep writing
even when I suspect myself
of emerging
with my words.

Park Date

My problem with being emotionally loyal in a relationship
is that often the past still hangs around my mind
on the park benches
not involved in the dog walking
or the games of frisbee
just sitting
watching.

Crumpled Pieces

Do you take your mind
out of your pocket
when you're alone
and sometimes discover
that pieces of me
are crumpled inside it?

After the Party I

Climb up into myself for a while.
Peer through the branches.
See if anyone else has abandoned ground.
Admire the view of glazed thought.
Listen to the murmured confessions of empty treehouses.
Close my eyes so we can watch each other from this height.

To the boy I thought I was in love with because he wasn't in love with me

You're like an ocean
I believed to be bottomless
that turned out to be a puddle
just reflecting the sky.

You

Loving you
was like keeping pace with misery
and still getting lapped,
like seeking out meaning
and arriving at the liquor store,
like watering a tree
after chopping up its roots.

Loving you
was how I began
to uproot my belief
that love would explain
itself to me
and never
me to it.

Unsharpened Pencils

It excites me to think that my person is somewhere out there,
maybe around the next corner I trip over,
maybe waiting for me by the water,
pen and paper in hand.

I like to think they will look up
as I pull out my stained journal
and unsharpened pencil
and they will say,

Yes, I was thinking it was about time for us to meet.

Globus Sensation

When I first wrote down Globus
it autocorrected to Goodbye
then Globud.

Globus Sensation is,
according to Google,
the result of the body preparing
for the physical release of crying
so it's good to know that both of us found release
from our ménage à un.

Crying,
according to Google,
acts as a social signal to elicit
empathy
and support from others
and, did you know,
says Google,
that crying can foster social connections
and strengthen bonds between people,

and, did you know,
says Google,
that if a tree falls in a forest
whether or not it makes a sound
depends upon your definition
of what it means to make a sound.

   A) if "sound" refers to physical vibrations
       then yes

   B) if "sound" implies a conscious perception by a listener
       then no

and, did you know,
says Google,
because given your search history
I feel like you definitely don't,
that if you cry by yourself in a forest
and no one is around to hear it
then that means that—
also,
here are some mental health resources
and know that you are not alone
unless of course you are
in which case, well,
to answer your question—

no one is listening.

Every Single Tree

My nothings
have always been more
than all of my
everythings
and I am the woods I got lost in
but I once believed someone
when they told me
they were every single tree.

Houseguest

Some memories will show up
with muddy shoes
that trample on your carpet
and red wine
that stains your couch
and a grinning reminder
that while you were
moving across state lines
and dyeing your hair
and tattooing your skin
and locking bathroom doors
and spilling ash trays
and perusing liquor aisles
and falling in lust
they have been there
watching
knowing that one day
you will have to look back.

Sticky Note

My problem is I'll take a crumb
and turn it into a bakery
and set the whole place on fire.

Tie-Dyed Love

My first romantic love
left me with many questions
about its prescriptive nature.
The thing with firsts
is they are often
relative.

On the first nondate he tells me
he doesn't want anything serious,
and on the second we fill a hiking trail
with messy, polysemous sex,
but on the third he tells me how beautiful
I look covered in sunlight,
and on the fourth that he is falling
in no particular direction,
and I wonder how quickly he found me synonymous
with that which he did not want.

I can't recall the coordinates
of the rendezvous that became a date,
but I know it was a formal, three-piece conversation,
and I know a late-night Uber
once took us both to a lake,
because one of us approached driving
with too much confidence,
and the other decided never
to approach it at all,
and I know I wondered how long falling

rather than being
could maintain its distinction.

Suddenly he is picking me up and dancing me on his feet,
he is telling me about his losses
and I am telling him about my absence of gains,
and I wonder at how we pretended
to grasp functionality
after comparing addictions
when we used all four hands
to hold everything but ourselves.

On bring-a-loved-one day
I introduced him to a floral couch,
overstuffed with mapless navigators
momentarily stirred
by the source of the peach-sized hickey
that walked in with a grin
one obscure summer day,
and I wonder how *I love you*
became something to double-check.

The day he tells me he's falling in love with me
he gives me his oldest, most beloved tie-dye sweater
to wear home,
years of love borne into tattered sleeves,
and I wonder if maybe this is what love looks like
after years,
vibrant, frayed, oversized,
and full of unexpected pockets.

Poetry

Poetry
for the memories I keep
in my back pocket
just in case.

About the Author

Dory Warner is an author and staunch feminist based in New York City. She writes primarily young adult fiction and poetry, both of which she does with hefty assistance from her pug, Norbert. Two years ago she made herself a promise: to finish her poetry manuscript. *Grippy Socks* is the fulfillment of that promise. Last year she left her full-time job and now balances two part-time jobs with her writing. She is currently at work on a young adult thriller.

www.ingramcontent.com/pod-product-compliance
Lightning Source LLC
Chambersburg PA
CBHW021254200426
R18167700001B/R181677PG43193CBX00002B/3